Endorsement for Waiting... on the Lord

The Life Factor
—**Daniel & Nadeen Wynter**

***

This book is so wholesome! The calming approach of truth and patience is suited well for a child to understand and deep enough for an adult to accept. This is great literature for a home to build strong kingdom foundations as it is an easy approach for families to gather in fellowship and conversation. Super inspiring and encouraging. Love this and I'm excited to share with family and friends, especially to those beginning their walk with Christ. I'm so proud of you Sam. This was an honor and pleasure to read. I love you and I'm so happy for you. Great job.
—**Angelica Diaz**, FAVOREIGN Inc..

***

In today's world, adults and children are programmed to have most things delivered to them instantly- "the microwave generation. "As a mother of 10 children ranging in ages from 6-28, I have observed the impact societal changes have created with ADD, and anxiety being diagnosed at an alarming rate. Children of today and of tomorrow will experience a great deal of anxiety if not taught the sound Biblical principles that *Waiting on The Lord* teaches with such immense power. Where, it shows how utilizing the stories from/in the Bible, of great men who had to wait on the Lord to see His grace operate in their lives. Now more than ever children and adults need to be reminded of the importance of developing and exercising patience. *Waiting on The Lord* teaches these essential principles with simplicity for young children to receive.
I am so very proud and honored to endorse *Waiting on The Lord*.
Blessings Always,
—**Nalish Francis**, FORVAN Financial Firm Inc.

***

This generation has normalized so many things that shouldn't have been thought to normalize. From music, to movies, to clothing, and more. We live in a "stop and go" world. This book allows young children to break the normalization of society and follow the path of who God wants us to be in this world.
Waiting on the Lord is teaching and showing patience, love, kindness, gratitude, and so much more.
I am extremely grateful to endorse *Waiting on the Lord*.
May the Lord Bless you.
—**Natasha Cherubino**, 888angelzzz

***

I love this book since it helps to shape the mindset of children to believe in the power of waiting on God's perfect timing in preparation for the triumphs and trials to come on their life journeys. As the children read this book, it will plant the seed which will be nourished with God's word for them to believe God is the gift! Waiting on God is less about waiting for your life circumstances to change and all about the TRANSFORMATIVE journey he takes you through to BECOME more like Jesus! I highly recommend this book for your little ones… they are our next generation of change-makers, apostles, prophets, teachers, pastors, preachers, and evangelists!
—**Millicent Dampare**, Papergirltoceo Consulting Inc.

Waiting... on The Lord

By: Samantha Maria Robinson

Published by KHARIS PUBLISHING, an imprint of KHARIS MEDIA LLC.

Copyright © 2025 Samantha Maria Robinson

ISBN-13: 978-1-63746-313-0

ISBN-10: 1-63746-313-8

Library of Congress Control Number: 2025932928

samantha.m.robinson@outlook.com

layouts, and text design by Samantha Robinson

All rights reserved. This book or parts thereof may not be reproduced in any form, stored in a retrieval system, or transmitted in any form by any means - electronic, mechanical, photocopy, recording, or otherwise - without prior written permission of the publisher, except as provided by United States of America copyright law.

Scripture quotations from The Authorized (King James) Version. Rights in the Authorized Version in the United Kingdom are vested in the Crown. Reproduced by permission of the Crown's patentee, Cambridge University Press

Scripture quotations marked NLT are taken from the Holy Bible, New Living Translation, Copyright © 1996, 2004, 2015 by Tyndale House Foundation. Used by permission of Tyndale House Publishers, Inc., Carol Stream, Illinois 60188. All rights reserved.

Scripture quotations marked (ESV) are from the ESV® Bible (The Holy Bible, English Standard Version®), © 2001 by Crossway, a publishing ministry of Good News Publishers. Used by permission. All rights reserved. The ESV text may not be quoted in any publication made available to the public by a Creative Commons license. The ESV may not be translated in whole or in part into any other language

All KHARIS PUBLISHING products are available at special quantity discounts for bulk purchase for sales promotions, premiums, fund-raising, and educational needs. For details, contact:

Kharis Media LLC
Tel: 1-630-909-3405
support@kharispublishing.com
www.kharispublishing.com

Dedication

This book is dedicated to my dad, Apostle Daniel Wynter; who was used by God to instruct me on publishing my books. He loved all his children and by Holy Spirit, taught me everything I know. With his teachings of knowledge and revelations, I am able to pass them on to the children in my class and all around the world.

Thank you.

This Book Belongs To:

_____

Lamentations 3: 25-26 KJV

The Lord is good unto them that wait for him, to the soul that seeketh him. It is good that a man should both hope and quietly wait for the salvation of the Lord.

Just like Abraham, I am waiting

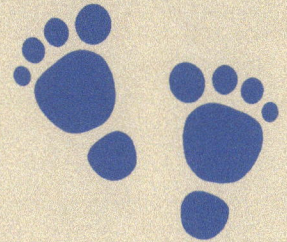

Just like Joseph, I am waiting

Just like David, I am waiting

Just like Moses, I am waiting

Hebrews 6:13-15 ESV

For when God made a promise to Abraham, since he had no one greater by whom to swear, he swore by himself, saying, "Surely I will bless you and multiply you." And thus Abraham, having patiently waited, obtained the promise.

Abraham waited for God to bless him since the Lord promised Abraham and Sarah a child and to make Abraham a great nation.

Genesis 39: 20-21 NLT

So he took Joseph and threw him into the prison where the king's prisoners were held, and there he remained. But the Lord was with Joseph in the prison and showed him his faithful love. And the Lord made Joseph a favorite with the prison warden.

Joseph waited on the Lord since God showed him in a dream that he would reign. Even while Joseph was a slave and was put in prison, he served God and was later moved from prison to Pharaoh's palace.

1 Samuel 16:12-13 NLT

So Jesse sent for him. He was dark and handsome, with beautiful eyes. And the Lord said, "This is the one; anoint him." So as David stood there among his brothers, Samuel took the flask of olive oil he had brought and anointed David with the oil. And the Spirit of the Lord came powerfully upon David from that day on.
Then Samuel returned to Ramah.

David had waited for God many times, including when he was anointed to be king but wasn't appointed until years later. While waiting, David continued to serve the Lord, whole-heartedly by serving Saul.

Exodus 24: 12-14 ESV

The Lord said to Moses, "Come up to me on the mountain and wait there, that I may give you the tablets of stone, with the law and the commandment, which I have written for their instruction." So Moses rose with his assistant Joshua, and Moses went up into the mountain of God. And he said to the elders, "Wait here for us until we return to you. And behold, Aaron and Hur are with you. Whoever has a dispute, let him go to them."

Moses waited for God to bring him into the promise land. While he waited for this promise, the Lord had Moses wait on other occasions, like on the mountain; waiting to receive the law.

Psalm 40: 1-3 KJV

I waited patiently for the Lord; and he inclined unto me, and heard my cry. He brought me up also out of an horrible pit, out of the miry clay, and set my feet upon a rock, and established my goings. And he hath put a new song in my mouth, even praise unto our God: many shall see it, and fear, and shall trust in the Lord.

Waiting for God could be hard. As we wait for the Lord, we must wait patiently while believing and trusting that He will work everything out.

While waiting for the Lord, it is important to serve, worship, pray, and give God thanks; Even if it feels like nothing is happening.

It is important to willingly give
God our best, even while we wait;
Always having Him in our hearts
and in our minds.

Isaiah 40:31 NLT

But those who trust in the Lord will find new strength. They will soar high on wings like eagles. They will run and not grow weary. They will walk and not faint.

As we wait, God is building us up by increasing our hope and renewing our strength.

Micah 7:7 ESV

But as for me, I will look to the Lord; I will wait for the God of my salvation; my God will hear me.

The Lord hears all of our prayers and He will answer them all in His perfect timing.

Psalm 37:3-5 NLT

Trust in the Lord and do good. Then you will live safely in the land and prosper. Take delight in the Lord, and he will give you your heart's desires. Commit everything you do to the Lord. Trust him, and he will help you.

While waiting to receive answers from God, we must have faith; Believing He will give us the desires of our hearts.

God is always moving on His children's behalf.

Even if we can't see, hear, or feel Him, the Lord is always working.

Sometimes His answers come quickly, and sometimes it may feel like they come slowly.

How ever long the wait may be, the Lord never stops working. So, wait patiently for the Lord...

...Because when God does answer your prayers, it is always worth the wait.

I wait patiently for Jesus, because He waits patiently for me.

Write about a time you waited for Jesus.

_____
_____
_____
_____
_____
_____
_____
_____

Waiting on God is Good!

Psalm 27:14 KJV

Wait on the Lord: be of good courage, and he shall strengthen thine heart: wait, I say, on the Lord.

Isaiah 30:18 KJV

And therefore will the Lord wait, that he may be gracious unto you, and therefore will he be exalted, that he may have mercy upon you: for the Lord is a God of judgment: blessed are all they that wait for him.

Psalm 33:20-21 NLT

We put our hope in the Lord. He is our help and our shield. In him our hearts rejoice, for we trust in his holy name.

Psalm 130:5-7 ESV

I wait for the Lord, my soul waits, and in his word I hope; my soul waits for the Lord more than watchmen for the morning, more than watchmen for the morning. O Israel, hope in the Lord! For with the Lord there is steadfast love, and with him is plentiful redemption.

Romans 8:24-25 NLT

We were given this hope when we were saved. (If we already have something, we don't need to hope for it. But if we look forward to something we don't yet have, we must wait patiently and confidently.)

Waiting... on the Lord

Waiting... on the Lord is a short storybook that teaches children about the importance of waiting on Jesus, what we need to do while we wait, and what God does while we are waiting. It includes biblical scriptures that explain how other individuals in the bible had to wait on God for their desires to come to pass. This book is designed for both children and adults to read together, allowing open conversations between the readers to take place.

By: Samantha Maria Robinson

About Kharis Publishing:

Kharis Publishing, an imprint of Kharis Media LLC, is a leading Christian and inspirational book publisher based in Aurora, Chicago metropolitan area, Illinois. Kharis' dual mission is to give voice to under-represented writers (including women and first-time authors) and equip orphans in developing countries with literacy tools. That is why, for each book sold, the publisher channels some of the proceeds into providing books and computers for orphanages in developing countries so that these kids may learn to read, dream, and grow. For a limited time, Kharis Publishing is accepting unsolicited queries for nonfiction (Christian, self-help, memoirs, business, health and wellness) from qualified leaders, professionals, pastors, and ministers. Learn more at: https://kharispublishing.com/

www.ingramcontent.com/pod-product-compliance
Lightning Source LLC
LaVergne TN
LVHW070058080426
835510LV00027B/3436